THE SOCIAL ENTREPRENEUR'S

A TO Z

ON ANXIETY, LEADERSHIP AND GETTING ENOUGH SLEEP

THE SOCIAL ENTREPRENEUR'S

ON ANXIETY, LEADERSHIP AND GETTING ENOUGH SLEEP

LIAM BLACK

FOREWORD BY PROFESSOR MUHAMMAD YUNUS

I dedicate this book to the memory of

Stephen Lloyd

(1951–2014)

lawyer, social entrepreneur, cyclist,
friend, all round good man

———

"Every business," he said,
"needs a maniac and a minder."

Thanks

Many thanks to the excellent Matter&Co team who brought
such flair and hard work to this project:
Tim West, Olivia Twaites, Alessandra Ellis, Sarah Furneaux and Sarah Gill.
The genius illustrator that is Spike Gerrell (landofspike.co.uk)
and to my scattered editorial board of lovely, clever people, namely,
Helen Trevaskis, Dr Zella King, Oliver Karius, Lisa Gansky and Julia Rebholz.

And, of course, as always, to Maggie.

Foreword

by Professor Muhammad Yunus

———

For more than 30 years, I have argued that capitalism as it is now is flawed. It is based on the false assumption that human beings are one-dimensional creatures interested only in selfish profit maximisation.

To address this basic flaw, we need to introduce a new kind of business – one that recognises the multi-dimensional nature of human beings. I call it the "social business" and I have devoted my life to creating such companies that can solve human problems, achieve scale and be financially viable.

I am very happy to see that more and more people are getting on board with the idea. We are seeing entrepreneurs throughout the world setting up social businesses, which are about achieving a specific social goal and not for personal gain.

A lot of young people are being inspired and mobilised by the emergence of significant social investment funds, by the growing coalition of cities, universities, corporations and regional bodies all taking the social business agenda seriously. This is a very good sign.

A key to the success of this movement is how we share our learning and support one another to start and grow social businesses. Liam Black, who I have known for many years, has been part of the social enterprise movement, creating businesses to do good, for more than 20 years.

In this A to Z – and I am very happy to see the letter "Y" dedicated to me! – Liam brings to social entrepreneurs his experience, wisdom, and insight, all delivered with his trademark directness and sense of humour to inform, encourage, educate and – when needed – admonish.

I hope you will read it, enjoy it, learn a lesson or two from it and then act to create, step by step, the world that we dream of – where not a single person remains poor.

Yunus
Dhaka, October 2014

Professor Muhammad Yunus is a multi-award winning social entrepreneur, the founder of the Grameen Bank and a Nobel Laureate.

An introduction

—

This publication started life as a speech to 150 young, would-be social entrepreneurs gathered in London in July 2013 to encourage and support one another. I was asked to run an honest, warts-and-all, hyperbole-free half an hour on my socially enterprising experiences. Encouraged by Tim West of Matter&Co I have put the stories into book form.

I want to speak directly to people – young and not so young – who want to make a difference in the world through enterprise. I have tried to distill my experiences over 25 years as founder, CEO, non-exec director, social investor, mentor and coach in social enterprise and in these pages you will find stories, top tips, advice, warnings, mea culpas.

Samuel Johnston (it's important to drop in a few literary references to bask in reflected wisdom – so here's my first) said that people need to be reminded much more than they need to be instructed.

Look elsewhere for grand theories of change or blinding new insights into business and entrepreneurship. And you will find no attempts at definitions. I have always believed that social enterprise is as social enterprise does.

In a book I wrote ten years ago with my great friend Jeremy Nicholls, *There's No Business Like Social Business,* we wrote:

"Social enterprise is a state of mind. It's about values, a passion for social justice and equity matched by the drive to create self-sufficient, market facing businesses."

If you call yourself a social entrepreneur – or you want to – that's good enough for me. Read on. If you get theological about all this stuff, well, this book probably isn't for you.

Starting any enterprise – social or otherwise – is bloody hard work and I can guarantee you will be stretched, challenged, terrified, exhilarated, knocked down, lifted up, bored – sometimes all in one working day! If you find just one thing within these pages which helps you on your socially entrepreneurial journey, the job of writing all this down will have been worthwhile.

Peace, love and profit

Liam
London, October 2014

Liam Black, Chief Encouragement Officer
Wavelength | @LiamABlack

A bit about me

Memory is a liar and like many social entrepreneurs I have created plenty of legends over 20 years – whilst also trying to make sense of life, earn a living and make a tiny dent in the profound injustices and inequalities of this world. But as spin free as I am able, this is my history relevant to this A to Z.

My social enterprise journey started in earnest at the Furniture Resource Centre (FRC) in Liverpool in the early 1990s. I joined the board of what was then a second-hand furniture charity and soon became chairman, taking over as CEO in 1997.

With co-founders Nic Frances and Robbie Davison we began re-inventing the organisation, moving it over several years from a charity reliant on donations and the kindness of strangers to a multi-million pound group of social businesses selling a range of products and services. In so doing, it created livelihoods for the long-term unemployed in a city battered by years of seismic economic change. Our company slogan was "We Do Good Things". And we really did. And ten years after I left, they still are.

FRC (a manufacturing and logistics business) gave birth to Create (a white goods recycling business), Revive (a furniture retailer), Bulky Bob's (a waste management company working in

partnership with the public sector) as well as numerous other business ideas that didn't make it past prototype. The Cat's Pyjamas was another venture, invented to deal with the legions of people who wanted to come to Merseyside to see what we were up to.

We welcomed many hundreds of social enterprise leaders, wannabe social entrepreneurs, Government policy makers and enterprise tourists. As well as working in the north west of England we ran learning events in the USA (Top Cat) and South Africa (Big Cat). During that time too I helped found the Social Enterprise Coalition (now called Social Enterprise UK) and sat on its board for a few years. I spoke at the launch of the Government's first social enterprise strategy at Number 10 Downing Street in July 2002 and served for three years as one of the UK Government's Social Enterprise Ambassadors.

In 2004 I published the book, *There's No Business Like Social Business*, with

Jeremy Nicholls and I moved south and took over the reins of Jamie Oliver's Fifteen restaurant brand. With a great team we opened businesses in Amsterdam, Melbourne and Cornwall. The goal was simple: open fantastic, top end restaurants and embed troubled youngsters in a world-class chef apprenticeship.

In 2008 I co-founded Wavelength with Adrian Simpson and Jessica Stack and this is what takes up most of my time and energy today.

I also help to pick winners for Impact Ventures UK and Centrica's Ignite fund. Together they are investing £40 million in social businesses in the UK. I mentor a number of hugely inspiring younger social entrepreneurs, write the Dear Jude blog on PioneersPost.com – and I can't pass a microphone without wanting to offer my opinion.

And so, ladies and gentlemen, *The Social Entrepreneur's A to Z* …

THE SOCIAL ENTREPRENEUR'S

A TO Z

ON ANXIETY, LEADERSHIP
AND GETTING ENOUGH SLEEP

is for

—

Anxiety

> "Anxiety's like a rocking chair.
> It gives you something to do,
> but it doesn't get you very far."
>
> Jodi Picoult, author

———

I remember like it was yesterday. The bowel melting worry when my financial director Tony told me our monthly salary bill had passed £40k: "That's lot of sofas to sell, Liam," he deadpanned.

I lay awake that night staring at the ceiling (in the spare room), my brain churning about the future of our social enterprise beside the banks of the Mersey. (*Christ. What if we don't achieve £40k? We'll have to let people go… What about all those unemployed guys we've recruited?… What will everyone say… about the business? About me?*) In and out of half sleep, coming wide-awake at 4am. (I don't know why but it is always around 4am for me!).

Creating, scaling and sustaining any enterprise is demanding and will really test you, so be prepared. Worry – and its pernicious first cousin, self-doubt – have been long-time companions of mine. You are in unknown territory so your mind will play all sorts of tricks on you.

A big cog in my anxiety generator has been the habit of comparing myself with others perceived as more successful, creative, happier, productive, famous.

Try not to do this. Everyone's success is unique. You never know the full story of their struggles, mistakes and huge strokes of luck. Believe me it is always a lot messier and contingent than it looks! "Insist on yourself," said Ralph Waldo Emerson. "Never imitate."

"Everyone's success is unique. You never know the full story of their struggles, mistakes and strokes of luck"

In my fifties the things I worry about have changed as my life circumstances have shifted. The worries you have with small kids – *Am I letting them down by not earning more money? Should I be at home more? Am I spending this last couple of decades of my working life the best way I can? Have I done my best work already?*

I am much better at managing anxiety and, for sure, once you've been round the block a few times, you have more to draw on to help deal with it. When you've made some monumental cock-ups in your career you learn that you do survive and, if you've been acting with integrity and authenticity, then people, by and large, are forgiving.

So, if you are feeling anxious about how to start your socially enterprising journey, panicking about cashflow or lying awake worrying about how you exit – take heart. Worry is part of the process of creation. Don't let it paralyse you, it might help keep you honest.

Fear – of failure, letting people down, losing money – can be a powerful fuel for your entrepreneurial drive. But it is deadly if you become driven by it.

is for

—

**Business Basics
(nail them)**

> "You can practise shooting eight hours a day, but if your technique is wrong, then all you become very good at is shooting the wrong way. Get the fundamentals down and the level of everything you do will rise."
>
> Michael Jordan, basketball legend

———

At the height of my messianic fervour about social enterprise in the late 1990s, I opened the *Liverpool Echo* newspaper and basked in the glory of an interview I gave in which my brilliant insights about enterprise and regeneration were laid out for all of Merseyside to see.

Social enterprise, I asserted – with all the confidence of the social entrepreneur with a few years of trading under his belt (some of them profitable) – was the powerful wind which would propel the city out of the doldrums. My wife said she was very impressed as she handed me a glass of red wine. And I think she was being sincere.

On returning to my office in the morning there was a piece of paper stuck to the door. It was from Stan Riley, one of the upholsterers and our trade union convenor: "Liam, I read in the *Echo* you will be transforming the city. You can't even get our wages right. Good luck with Liverpool."

Ouch. We had been having persistent problems in the finance team and many of the guys had not been getting the right wages and there were constant issues about tax codes. In a company where many of the workers were paid weekly in cash this is a big issue. In a social enterprise that was set up to offer secure work for the long-term unemployed this is a failure of mission.

I was intoxicated with my own rhetoric and liked being on stage much more than chasing down systems failures. I had forgotten to pay close enough attention to the dull but critically important basics of running a business. Many parts of running a business are indeed very dull and I've always been drawn to the big picture not the micro stuff. But this has caught me out many times. Stan's laconic note is the best reminder I've had about leadership hubris.

"Liam, I read in the *Echo* you will be transforming the city. You can't even get our wages right. Good luck with Liverpool"

By all means aspire to change the world but make sure the vehicle you are using to drive that change has an engine that works!

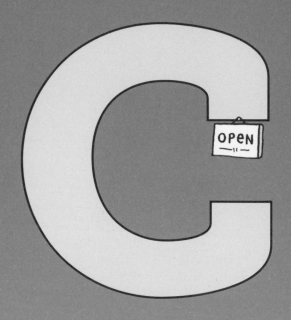

is for
—
Customers

> "Repetition makes reputation and reputation makes customers."
>
> Elizabeth Arden, entrepreneur

———

The shop looked brilliant. The staff had shiny new uniforms; the furniture was carefully arranged and sparkled with 'buy me' loveliness. It looked for all the world that the hundreds of thousands of pounds we had spent to refurbish and launch this retail revolution had been well used to bring Liverpool's low-income shoppers a great new offer.

Trouble was, none of the thousands of working class Liverpudlians tumbling off the buses outside the store wanted to buy any of it. They'd come in, stay for a few seconds and leave. And the till remained untroubled by cash. For weeks on end. Board meetings were like walking on broken glass as I tried ever more elaborate explanations for why we were gushing money and failing spectacularly to hit our social objectives.

We had got carried away with our own certainties about our socially enterprising brilliance and not really listened to the people we wanted to shop with us. We assumed that if we spent enough money and really, really wanted it to work, then it would. It didn't.

We opened this enterprise – Revive – at the height of the success of the other businesses in the FRC Group when we thought we could do no wrong.

"We had got carried away with our own certainties about our socially enterprising brilliance"

We wasted a lot of money and would have had a bigger social impact if we'd just handed out envelopes of cash to people as they got off the buses!

But the plain truth is that we – I – had not spent the time to understand what our target customer base really wanted and whether they would pay for what we had to sell them. We had, as a leadership team, drifted away from the times and places where our customers gathered. This is a fatal error.

Ian Galbraith was my congenitally sceptical logistics manager in Liverpool who would roll his eyes at my latest wheezes. His core belief was that people at the top of a company have no real idea what goes on with customers and, worse, pretend they do and always overstate how good the service is. In his memory I present the Galbraith Hypothesis:

The degree of confidence in the quality of a service is inversely proportional to your distance from the front line.

So, get close to your front line regularly and see, feel, know how your service is experienced by your customers and beneficiaries.

D

is for

—

Don't believe the hype!

"How many social entrepreneurs does it take to change a light bulb? One. And a committee of 12 of the great and good to hand over the 'You're SO Awesome Award'."

Jude Noir, social entrepreneur

———

Have you won a social enterprise award yet? If not don't worry, there will be another competition you can enter coming along any minute.

It is entirely possible to spend your life schlepping from one social entrepreneur conference to another being told by politicians/celebrities/actors/wealthy Americans/former presidents just how bloody amazing you are. Indeed, some of the social entrepreneurs who breathe the rarefied air in Oxford University's Skoll World Forum or the World Economic Forum in Davos seem to spend all their time talking about the poor in five star hotels to the ever-so concerned rich and pained. Building a personal brand, one kiss-up at a time.

If poverty could be ended by the hot air generated in Oxford and Davos they'd be bathing in caviar in the slums of Rio and Nairobi tonight.

The social entrepreneur awards culture has been fascinating to watch develop. With the arrival of the Skoll and Schwab big bucks, those who are elevated to the ranks of fellows receive substantial cash – and a world of C-suite access and connectivity opens up.

The social entrepreneur PR industry grows all the time and is hungry for content and personalities. This is dangerous and results in people being hailed as saviours and game changers when their business models are nowhere near proven – still less their damaging, unintended consequences known and understood.

Skoll et al have brought many great things to the sector and their contributions to the developing eco-system are huge. But the creation of a super league of A-list celebrity social entrepreneurs, networking, dining behind the VIP curtain is not without its contradictions and problems.

Certain of those A-listers are bullshitters and narcissists whose mission is themselves. I have looked behind the scenes of a few of their ventures and the mismatch between rhetoric and reality is stark – as is the misalignment between personal lifestyle and public stance about the poor and oppressed.

"Be your own fiercest critic. Take the issues of poverty and empowerment seriously but for goodness sake don't take yourself too seriously and never believe what is said or written about you"

Be your own fiercest critic. Take the issues of poverty and empowerment seriously but for goodness sake don't take yourself too seriously and never believe what is said or written about you.

is for
—
Evidence

> "What can be asserted without evidence
> can be dismissed without evidence."

Christopher Hitchens, contrarian

———

Social and environmental challenges are complex, messy, multi-dimensional, contested. Over claiming, confusing cause and effect, and not acknowledging unintended consequences are endemic across the non-profit sector.

So, how would you know you were having the impact you say you intend? Generating lots of activity is no evidence of impact. Scaling in itself is no sign of quality of impact. You may reach more people but quality is likely to suffer the bigger the spread.

One business I opened in Liverpool was Create, a recycler of fridges and washing machines to poor families. I pushed for increases in productivity to drive sales. This happened but so did a huge increase in complaints as washing machines flooded single mums' kitchens across the city. One metric was good – number of appliances saved from scrap – another was terrible – rightly furious customers who felt robbed of £35.

At Fifteen I commissioned a report on our work with young people. Everyone was expecting PR fluff so we thought we would confound critics with a blast of honesty. The findings in our report *Life in the Present Tense* were very mixed: we had missed the mark and let some youngsters down. But it made us change and improve.

"If your feedback loop is not making you wince then it is not working"

I have always found verification difficult, to cut through the noise to discern what really works and what is a pointless, tail-chasing exercise.

But investing that time and money to ask the right questions is an obligation on social entrepreneurs and, when done right, can radically improve performance.

Total commitment to impact verification is rare in the social entrepreneur world. When I was discussing this chapter with my old comrade Jeremy Nicholls – the social return on investment guru – he asked me a great question: "Have you ever heard of a social enterprise CEO being fired for failing to hit his or her social goals?" Actually, no. (If anyone reading this has, please get in touch.)

So, get really clear about your metrics and get someone with no financial or emotional stake in you to verify your results. Anecdotes and intentions are just not enough. If you come in front of me looking for investment I will want data.

And if your feedback loop is not making you wince, then it is not working.

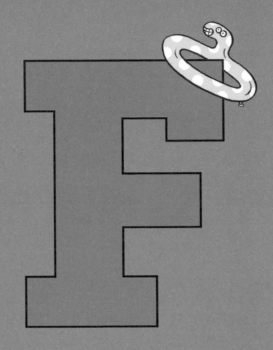

is for

—

Failure

> "If you have made mistakes, even serious ones, there is always another chance for you. What we call failure is not the falling down but the staying down."

Mary Pickford, actress

———

In the hyperbole drenched world of social entrepreneurship there is little space allowed for a grown up discussion about failure.

Today, driven by the super charged culture of Silicon Valley, there is a fetishisation of failure: "Fail forward, fail fast, failure is the best teacher." True enough failure can be a great teacher – if you're listening. But the best indicator of whether someone will be successful in a new business is if they have had a successful venture before – not how many times they have failed.

If a Silicon Valley geek fails to sell his start up to Google, well, tough, he will be disappointed but life will go on. Failure in a homeless organisation, a microfinance initiative, an employment project for young people has much, much more serious consequences – for people often least able to cope.

I have always hated failure and found it difficult to deal with. It is just bloody awful to see hard work and great intentions to change the world founder through lack of money, stupid management decisions, design flaws, terrible governance or my boneheaded pride.

I have many times proven to be a poor learner from my failures – only too happy to bury the bad news and walk on hoping no-one notices. In large part this is about ego and reputation – I don't want to be associated with failure, I'm a winner, I'm a social entrepreneur!

"If it's someone else's cash down the Swanee you're much more likely to spin the truth. At least I have"

I have seen social enterprises fail and as a result vulnerable people get put out on the street again or painstaking attempts to build confidence are shattered. That's not a learning opportunity – that's a huge failure of mission.

When I led larger businesses and failure happened in a team I was not managing or in another part of the world – that's when it becomes really hard to learn from failure. Too many egos, too much back covering, too much politics going on. The culture – and too often me – shrugs and is just all too happy to bury the bad news, spin it positively to the board, pretend to learn something and move on. This is especially easy in the "non-profit" environment when money lost isn't felt personally. If it's someone else's cash down the Swanee you're much more likely to spin the truth. At least I have.

So, you must learn how to live with failure, how to minimise the damage, expect it to hurt, and learn as much as you can and talk openly about it – but don't wear it as a badge of honour.

is for

—

GO!

> "If you want a happy ending,
> that depends, of course,
> on where you stop your story."

Orson Welles, film director

———

In social entrepreneurship, leaving well, at the right time, with the organisation in rude health, can be a very tricky exercise.

In a straight, for-profit business the exit options are obvious for the successful founding entrepreneur. Start it, grow it, sell it and move on. Start something else, become an EOB (Entrepreneur on the Beach) or angel investor, write a book, front a terrible TV show. In the non-profit world the cash-out exit door is locked.

I have seen too many promising social businesses stall or begin to rot because the founding social entrepreneur has insufficient self-awareness to know when it is the right time to leave. Starting something and growing something to scale require very different skill sets and experience.

Beware building an organisation in your image, a platform for your ego, which is all but impossible for you to leave because if you do it will fold. Build your company not just your profile.

Not every social entrepreneur is a good leader. Why should they be? Indeed, the wholly unrealistic expectations we have of social entrepreneurs (be innovative, business savvy, charismatic and a great CEO/leader) set up many for burn out and failure to realise early promise.

"Starting something and growing something to scale require very different skill sets and experience"

Start up, although fraught with challenges and worry, is exciting and pushes all your buttons. Managing a larger company with all the DBI (dull but important) stuff to be done (tax, legals, governance, HR) may not be for you – probably isn't. So, at the very outset, start thinking about what your exit might look like. Be honest with yourself. You might be the fire starter but not want to be a CEO. That's absolutely fine but be clear with the people around you – especially your board – what your intentions are and how you want your role to develop as the enterprise grows and changes.

Don't let your ego and lack of insight get in the way of the successful scaling and maturing of the great thing you started.

H
is for
—
Hire slowly, fire quickly

> **"Culture isn't part of the game it IS the game."**
>
> Lou Gerstner, former CEO, IBM

———

The biggest mistakes I have made in my career have been in hiring the wrong people and not moving quickly enough to deal with poor performing leaders. I have wasted hundreds of thousands of pounds and too much of my life on getting to the exit people I let in who just don't fit or – worse – became cultural terrorists undermining the kind of enterprise I wanted to create.

As FRC grew in Liverpool I would spend ages poring over the specifications of the fleets of lorries we were leasing. We'd get lawyers to crawl through the small print, negotiate hard to get the best deal, road test them, and complain and ask for refunds very quickly when there were problems. Yet we would let people into senior management roles after a couple of interviews and a cursory glance at references. A broken down lorry is a problem which is easily fixed; an underperforming senior leader who can't or won't align with the values of the business is so much more serious and can cause enormous damage.

I can't overstate the importance of getting the right people around you. When you can gather all your team in one small room it's easy to keep the culture strong and aligned. But as you grow and you no longer see your co-leaders as regularly this is when the rot can set in.

It took me years to understand that a strong, high performing culture comes from having aligned leadership behind a shared mission. All it takes is one member of the senior team to be out of step and cynicism and underperformance are not far behind.

I like the 'Law of Three' when it comes to recruitment. For any important vacancy, always interview at least three candidates, three times and involve three colleagues in the interview who must be unanimous before an appointment can be made.

At Zappos.com, if you successfully complete the company's induction, founder Tony Hsieh will offer you a big cheque and a great reference should you wish to leave at that point rather than take up the job. He wants only those who are passionate about his enterprise's mission. He had to increase the offer from $2,000 to $5,000 because too few were taking it! And never forget the golden rule on hiring: a 'Don't know' is a 'No'.

"A strong, high performing culture comes from having aligned leadership behind a shared mission"

Take the greatest of care with the health of your culture. Unaligned senior managers are an infection and you must be the penicillin.

is for

—

Innovation

> **"A good plan violently executed now is better than a perfect plan executed next week."**
>
> George Patton, US army general

Innovation is these days a fairly meaningless word. It's like sex and teenage boys. They all talk about it but few are doing it. (Or was that just my generation?) In London you could spend every day going to a 'workshop' run by an innovation foundation and never actually start anything.

Creativity and new ideas are crucial but they're nothing without the resources and culture that enable ruthless execution. Never forget an idea only becomes an innovation when someone buys it. Maybe this chapter should have been 'I is for Incredibly focused on getting shit done'

because without such focus 'innovation' is merely creative masturbation.

Google's Law of Failure states that eight out of ten innovations will fail – even when brilliantly executed. So the question is not "How do I avoid failure?" but "How do I fail quickly and move on with as little damage done as possible?"

I really like the 'pretotyping' approach to innovation – championed by Google guru Alberto Savoia – which attempts to verify the market appeal of a product or service at the lowest possible price and in the least amount of time. It is as appropriate for the hungriest, cash strapped social enterprise start-up as it is for the deep pocketed multinational.*

Alberto's manifesto is worth pinning on your wall: *Innovators beat ideas, pretotypes beat productypes, building beats talking, simplicity beats features, now beats later, commitment beats committees, data beats opinions.*

"Now beats later, commitment beats committees, data beats opinions"

So, test your ideas ideas quickly and inexpensively with simplified versions of your product to validate the premise: that, "If we build it, they will use it." How I wish I had done this with the Revive retail concept I mentioned earlier. I built it and they bloody well did not come!

Get over any sense that you can create the finished article early on. You can't. In the immortal words of Ernest Hemingway: "The first draft of anything is shit."

And never underestimate the power of a commitment to relentless, incrementalist innovation. Sudden radical change is rare. Lasting change is more often wrought by multiple smaller acts of creativity and bravery underpinned by deep patience and resilience – sometimes grinding it out inch by hard won inch.

"It's not that I'm so smart," quipped Einstein. "It's just that I stay with problems longer."

* www.pretotyping.org

52

is for

—

Jump!

"There is a difference between knowing
the path and walking the path."

Morpheus, *The Matrix*

―――――

No matter how great your ideas, they mean nothing until you act on them. The willingness to start, to jump, to take that first step without all the answers is what separates the entrepreneurs and changemakers from the poseurs and wannabes.

There is never a perfect time. There will always be the need for more data and evidence. There will always be what looks like a good reason to wait. There will always be that little voice in your brain telling you that you're mad and you will surely fail and look like an idiot.

In my late forties I left a well paid, high profile, high status CEO role to hold hands with two mates and jump into the unknown to start Wavelength. Why? (My wife asked this question a lot). Partly I'd had it with the pressures of running Fifteen, the board politics, and the travel. But I was getting bored too and wanted something different, unknown, to create, to start again. There is a devil in me that every few years whispers, "Liam, let's get out of here, walk away. It's not broken so let's break it."

Every social entrepreneur I've known well has a demon inside them, something a bit unhinged, unreasonable, restless. That touch of madness compelling them to chase their passions and choose uncertainty, stress, relentless uphillness, sleepless nights and the high probability of failure that comes with starting an enterprise.

"There will always be that little voice in your brain telling you that you're mad"

The plummet after my jump six years ago often made me sick with worry as we struggled to find the right business model to deliver our vision before our money ran out.

The comfort of a guaranteed monthly salary, the predictabilities of an established company, the attention the role attracted – losing all this came as a shock to me. I didn't realise until I stepped out of it how far I had allowed that role to underpin my sense of who I was: "If you're no longer the leader of the UK's best known social enterprise, Liam, what are you?"

But we found our wings before we hit the ground and we are still airborne. By taking that first step forward things changed, the world looked different, new angles appeared, new allies could see us, and new opportunities came to us. If you stand still you can't see new opportunities – and they can't see you.

So if your journey has brought you to the edge of the cliff, peering over into the unknown, take a few steps back, take a deep breath and run forward! Geronimo!

As Goethe may (or may not) have said:
Are you in earnest?
Seize this very minute;
What you can do, or dream you can do,
Begin it;
Boldness has genius, power
And magic in it.

K

is for

—

Know yourself

"Commandment #1: Believe in yourself.
Commandment #2: Get over yourself."

Kristan Higgins, writer

———

What really – really – drives you and what do you want? If you want to be socially enterprising over the long haul, understanding what motivates you is crucial.

In today's cult of the busy and preternaturally brilliant entrepreneur there is little time for honesty about real motives and desires. If you'd asked me in my twenties and thirties what my driving motivations were I would have outlined a strange hybrid of left wing politics, option-for-the-poor Catholicism and Irish republicanism.

No doubt that these were important to me. But looking back at that needy, driven, contradictory young man I can see clearly that a core part of what drove him was seeking the approval of an absent father (long story)*. *Look at me, Dad, helping all these homeless people, aren't I great? Aren't I?*

And, to be frank, I hugely enjoyed the attention which came with being in the vanguard of the UK social enterprise movement. It feels very good to be talked and written about and even better if there are awards and baubles. (And look at me now in middle age wanting you to love this book and tell me I'm needed.) There may well be no 'I' in 'team' but there is sure as hell a lot of 'ego' in 'social entrepreneur'.

A word of caution to all those middle class, European and American social entrepreneurs who think they have the answer for the problems of Africa or know what the youth off the housing estates need: You don't. Do Kenyans and Cambodians really need more over-educated university graduates from Oxford and Stanford working out their own issues through the belief they are social entrepreneurs?

The Brazilian priest and champion of the poor Helder Camara once said: "The poor are not the raw material of your salvation." This is for all of us to tattoo on our foreheads (whether we do God or not).

It's messy this social entrepreneurship thing, this mix of personal ambition, neediness, the desire to save, to do good, to be known, recognised, rewarded, happy, useful. But try to know why you do what you do and temper your passion to change the world with a large dose of humility.

"There may well be no 'I' in 'team' but there is sure as hell a lot of 'ego' in 'social entrepreneur'"

* There is a whole book to be written about male social entrepreneurs and their fathers. Every single one I've mentored has had a very complicated relationship with their dads and the need to impress them and seek their approval for their socially entrepreneurial heroics.

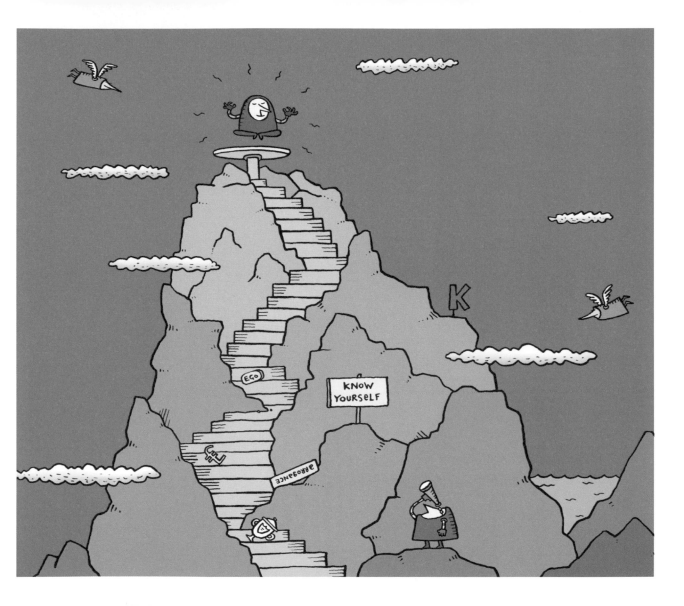

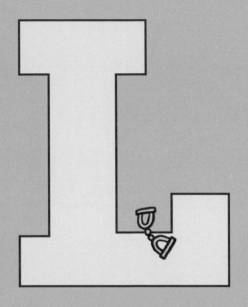

is for

—

Look after yourself

"Whatever is bringing you down, get rid of it.
Because you'll find that when you're free, your true creativity,
your true self comes out."

Tina Turner, goddess

———

When I start mentoring a social entrepreneur my first piece of advice is usually: "Book a holiday and get laid." Not very profound I know but social entrepreneurs always believe they are indispensable and their work so important that the world will stop turning if they take a week in Greece.

How effective do you think you are really being after working seven days a week flat out for a year? People who are jaded, knackered, running on empty are not very productive and rubbish role models for the people they lead.

And surprise, surprise – their relationships suffer. Plenty of marriages have foundered on the rocks of the social entrepreneur's driven-ness and willingness to save the world and not their relationships.

Building anything – let alone something as tough as a profitable social enterprise – requires commitment, a probably unhealthy dose of self-belief, the ability to be knocked down ten times and get up eleven – and the insight to know when to step back, recuperate and recharge.

There is a reason why they tell you on a plane to put the mask over your face first before helping others. If you're not breathing you can't help.

"Look after yourself and your relationships. It's good for business. And, who knows, you might get more sex"

The good news though for all the workaholic narcissists out there is that looking after yourself *is* good for business and achieving high performance. I have had some of my best ideas and insights whilst out walking the dog or running. Don't believe me? Stanford University worked out that a person's creative output increased by an average of 60 percent when walking. Peter Keen, an architect of Team GB's cycling success at London 2012, says that getting off the bike – literally and metaphorically – and slowing right down, going for a walk alone, is a critical part of maintaining high performance. "Learning quicker by thinking slower," is how Peter frames it.

People can be divided into energy makers and energy takers. Purge the cynics and naysayers from your life. "Keep away from people who try to belittle your ambitions," advised Mark Twain. "Small people always do that, but the really great make you feel that you, too, can become great."

And a word on meetings. If you have to have them – and in my experience the more meetings I have the less effective I am – don't rush from one to another. Give yourself at least half an hour between them to process and get your head straight. And don't have more than three a day.

So, look after yourself and your relationships. It's good for business. And, who knows, you might get more sex.

is for

—

Mentor

> "I am listening for what it is that you love to do.
> Because that's what you'll be best at."
>
> Ronnie Hughes, mentor

———

What is a mentor? Best definition I've come across is: "A wise and trusted counsellor or teacher. An influential senior sponsor or supporter or champion."

I have been really very fortunate with the mentors who have come into my life. In 1997 I recruited Graham Morris to the board of FRC. He had recently stepped out of a glittering career in the car industry where he had operated at the highest levels, finishing his time as the boss of Rolls Royce and Bentley. He had more business knowledge and commercial acumen in his little finger than I had in my whole body and yet he was able to deploy it and help me learn without condescension or undermining me in my first CEO role.

Ronnie Hughes, with his sandals and beard, could not have been a more different character to Graham! He left social housing to set up as a life coach and social enterprise developer. But he was great for me too, helping me weather the emotional and personal resilience challenges which come when you take over the hot seat. His support and gentle but persistent questioning of my motives and responses was invaluable and helped get me through some very tough times.

I doubt either Graham or Ronnie appreciate the value of the hours we spent talking before FRC board meetings or just walking the streets of Liverpool.

My current adviser/mentor is again a very different sort of person from Graham and Ronnie, much younger than me and operating in an industry I never thought would be so helpful to me.

I have loved mentoring others, mainly younger social entrepreneurs. Sometimes it is about answering questions about business basics. Sometimes they have specific requests for introductions or resources. Sometimes they just want to be listened to about their fears and anxieties. Sometimes we just drink beer.

And how to get a good one? Think about why you need a mentor. Identify one – I got Graham by reading about him in the paper and writing to him. I noticed in the article he wanted to find a way of really helping Liverpool (his home city) so I told him I could help him with that and I needed his commercial nous.

"Mentor: A wise and trusted counsellor or teacher. An influential senior sponsor or supporter or champion"

So, just ask and be clear about what you want and what the commitment looks like. People like Graham are very busy and won't respond to vague requests. Help them help you by being specific.

is for

—

Networks

> "The good relationships and alliances you create define your mutual ability to be effective."
>
> Reid Hoffman, founder of LinkedIn

———

Business has always been as much about who you know as what you know and for the social entrepreneur this is so, so true. No one person, organisation, sector or industry has the solution for complex social and environmental problems. Your ability to create robust networks across systems which enable you to build, sell, fundraise, access supply chains, recruit, influence, will determine how effective you will be.

You must assemble and conduct an orchestra of people playing instruments who don't usually perform together. This takes time and applied intelligence.

Twitter and LinkedIn and the mushrooming of enterprise hubs and networks make cross sector alliances much easier to create and sustain than when I was starting out. (In the dark ages when there was no internet. Yes, children, that long ago.)

It is perilously easy to get stuck in your own social enterprise echo chamber. Make a point of going to events where you are not the centre of attention. One of the strengths of Wavelength for our social entrepreneur members is that they get to hang out with people from a very diverse range of businesses and backgrounds. They have chosen to put themselves in a much wider gene pool from which to draw learning and new connectivity.

"Serendipity is a huge part of anyone's success but you need to put yourself out there in order to help luck find you"

But don't allow your networking to become mere mingling, sipping warm white wine trying desperately to remember the name of the eejit you're stuck with in the corner.

The successful networker naturally seeks mutual benefit and is always thinking, "How can I enrich this network?" not, "What can I get out of these people?"

Serendipity is a huge part of anyone's success but you need to put yourself out there in order to help luck find you. Tim Smit – founder of the Eden Project – claims he accepts every third invitation no matter what it is. This he says forces him into unusual situations and helps serendipity happen. Extreme but he is structuring serendipity to his life. Find your way of doing that.

Be respectful and genuinely nice to PAs and secretaries – they are often much more influential over their bosses' diaries than you might imagine.

Enjoy yourself out there and manage those networks. And easy on the wine.

is for

—

Often

> **"Good habits are worth being fanatical about."**
>
> John Irving, writer

———

Often…

Say thank you.

Do this: every week send at least three thank you cards to people who have performed well, helped you out, added value to your life and business in some way. Hand write the cards and envelopes, use stamps – don't frank – and post first class on a Friday to their home addresses. I don't need to explain why, do I?

Learn about stuff which has nothing to do with your day-to-day business.

Don't become that obsessive who bangs on about his or her own business and is not interested in anyone else's story. Don't let your social enterprise consume you; one way of avoiding this is to take time to learn about something not directly relevant to your day-to-day concerns, with no obvious relevance to your change-the-world mission.

Ask yourself: "Am I really loving what I'm doing?"

Seriously, life is too short to be doing anything that doesn't completely engage and excite you.

Pay attention to the people who love you.

In *Bleak House*, there is a character called Mrs Jellyby. She's a tireless do-gooder for charitable projects in a far away country but doesn't notice her own family is falling apart around her. Dickens brilliantly skewers her as the "telescopic philanthropist".

"Seriously, life is too short to be doing anything that doesn't completely engage and excite you"

When I was CEO of Fifteen – a role that involved a lot of international travel – I arrived home late, jet-lagged and exhausted from a trip to Melbourne (for a three-hour board meeting), dying for my bed because I had to leave first thing for Amsterdam. As I walked into the house I had the awful realisation that I had missed my daughter's school parents' evening. She blanked me. As I tried lamely to apologise and make excuses to my wife Maggie, I broke eye contact and glanced down at the flashing red light on my BlackBerry. My beloved (of 30 years) then said something to me which really struck home: "Do you know the problem with you, Liam? You're never here and when you are here you're never here!"

I've hated BlackBerrys ever since.

P

is for

—

Profit

> "Money can't buy you happiness.
> But it can buy you a big yacht
> to pull up right alongside it."

David Lee Roth, rock star

———

In the mid 90s when I gave speeches all over Britain about our social enterprise experiment in Liverpool and what we were learning about the tricky balancing of social and commercial imperatives, I would ask the audience to stand, take a deep breath, and say after me: "Profit is good!"

Most of the crowd would stay sitting with arms firmly crossed, a few would venture to their feet slowly and mumble and others would shout "Shame!" or "Sell out!" A particularly angry community worker in Newcastle threw a shoe at me. He missed.

Today it is very different and all shades of opinion from the sandal-wearing co-op development worker to the Hugo Boss-suited ex-merchant banker accept the need for sustainable business models and the organisational health which regular cash surpluses help to create.

But how much of the value created by social entrepreneurs is it okay for them to take out? There is a lot of dancing round the handbags on this topic.

The money versus mission and purpose conundrum is easier to answer when you are in your twenties and thirties and certainly when you have no kids. Passion, mission, the feeling of making a difference in the world, proving that the profit motive is not the be all and end all – these are more important than making money, building a pension, saving for your kids' education.

But certainly for me as I got older I did reflect on all the financial value I was creating and how little of that I was getting. And the balance felt wrong to me.

I want to make more than a salary and be able to earn more if I work harder and grow a business. I believe I can do that and add lots of social value in the world. This issue is fiercely debated, long and hard, in the bars at social entrepreneur gatherings. At one extreme are the "Personal profit poisons everything" asset lockers; at the other are the "Let the market rip and if you pay peanuts you get monkeys" types.

We can argue all day about where the line is to be drawn but make sure you start thinking early on about your relationship with money and what is enough for you. Think very hard about what type of business you want to build and be honest with yourself, your partners and other stakeholders.

"Make sure you start thinking early on about your relationship with money and what is enough for you"

The worst thing to do is to drift along not resolving it and end up in resentful middle age. And as Woody Allen said, "Money is better than poverty, if only for financial reasons."

is for

—

Quality

> **"Quality is the best business plan."**
>
> John Lasseter, Woody's dad

———

At Fifteen in London we served more than 100,000 guests every year.

We had all sorts – boisterous city boys, anally retentive, fault finding foodies, JOTBs (Jamie Oliver True Believers), tourists who had planned their UK vacation around a table in Westland Place, and loads of couples from all over the country who had saved up their money to come and have their first meal at a fancy London restaurant to celebrate their wedding anniversaries or special birthdays.

The one thing that they had in common was the expectation that they were going to have a brilliant experience – and given that many of them were paying over £100 that is understandable. Keeping the quality of the food and service high was a daily challenge – especially for the chefs who also had to train and mentor our young apprentices (who were neither use nor ornament in the kitchen when they first started).

We wanted people first of all to have a great experience – and then feel good about themselves for coming to our restaurant and helping out the youth. We did not want to build the business on the pity purchase. We wanted them to keep coming back and spending money – buying that extra bottle of wine they didn't really plan to – because that is how we made more money to fund the apprenticeships. And telling their mates and family how great it is, not how worthy a cause it is.

"Set the bar high and then set it higher"

The food business is second only to the sex industry in terms of the intimacy of the experience. And pretty much as soon as that plate arrives in front of you, you know if it is any good or not.

Consistency is the key. No good being great one night and mediocre or rubbish the next. Think of the brands you love. John Lewis? Apple? Chances are what you love about them is not just that they provide high quality but that they do it again and again. Providing world-class products and services is the expected norm not an aspirational goal. You can *rely* on them for quality.

Think of your enterprise. Is it providing unmatched quality? Are you really proud of its ability to get it right time after time? John Lewis and Apple are only trying to flog stuff. YOU are trying to help the poor, aren't you? Set the bar high and then set it higher.

is for

—

Risk

> "I went to the butchers the other day and I bet him 50 quid
> that he couldn't reach the meat off the top shelf.
> He said, 'No, the steaks are too high.'"

Tommy Cooper, comedian

———

So, here's the deal. Create an enterprise that is financially viable and profitable in a space where the private and public sectors have failed. On the way to achieving your noble mission take on long-term unemployed people – many with a prison background – who do not have the skills and experience you need to run at optimal levels, increasing your costs and pushing your managers to the limit. This was pretty much the deal at both Fifteen and FRC. Sounds pretty risky, doesn't it?

Most people who start up a social enterprise are not risking any of their own money and often have free money given to them by foundations or other sources of philanthropy. True, they take some risks with their reputation and they might be able to earn more in a proper job but the risks are not as acute as the entrepreneur who remortgages his home or convinces her mother to put the family house up as collateral (as one of the women I've mentored did – she went bust and her mum lost £30,000!).

I was blessed at FRC with a first class board. One of them, Barry McKenzie – the CEO of a large bed manufacturer – would spend a lot of time walking the factory floors and warehouses talking to the upholsterers, drivers, fork lift truck guys – the people who made the place tick. Barry came to see me one day and shared his insight that the big split in our social enterprise was around appetite for risk. "You Liam want to change the world and are forever coming up with new ways to spend money and take a punt. Your shop floor staff want stability and to know they can pay their mortgages next year."

He was right. And of course if my initiatives and innovations didn't work out I could take off and start something else or get a well-paid job. The factory guys would be in a much worse position.

When you scale, the needs of the organisation become more and more consuming and it is very easy to lose sight of the purpose and mission and to settle into a very low risk strategy.

"Who takes the hit if the risks you take don't pay off?"

This is all very well if you sell widgets, but if your goal is to change things then taking risks is crucial. But who takes the hit if the risks you take don't pay off?

is for
—
Superhero
(sorry, you aren't one)

> **"What sort of leader are you really, Liam, because we have had some fucking shockers here before you."**
>
> Fifteen chef

———

A typically direct – and very good – question from one of the team at Fifteen when I joined the business as CEO. I cringe still at the naivety and stupidity I too often showed in the various leadership roles I have taken on.

There was my Messiah leadership phase ("Do this because you believe in me") in my twenties and early thirties. I had a vision of how the world would change and be a better place. Passion and belief are necessary to inspire and youthful idealism can be a powerful force. But the Messiah identity – very common amongst social entrepreneurs – makes disciples of the people around you and disciples are not known for their initiative.

Then there is the Superman leadership model: "Stand back – I can do it all". There are times when the leader needs to step in and show strength and courage. But over time this style of leadership is just too bloody tiring and does not draw on the talent and potential of the people around you. The social entrepreneur as superhero is, however, much applauded and rewarded by the social enterprise PR machine. But (whisper it) there are no superheroes – just flawed human beings in all our messiness, complexities, hang ups and narcissism.

And the third leadership identity I have inhabited – and tend to revert to in panic or times of stress – is the Stalin model: "Do it or else". Again, short and even medium term this can be a productive style but longer term it fails badly. It easily tips into bullying and deters talent from joining your business.

"I cringe still at the naivety and stupidity I too often showed in the various leadership roles I have taken on"

So be mindful of the sort of leader you want to be. Don't reach for a superhero's cape. If you do aspire to having a superpower, then make it the ability to create world-class teams.

Are leaders born or made? I don't know really but you can choose the behaviours you want to develop as a leader and then practise, practise, practise until it becomes your practice.

One of the leaders I most admire is Sue Campbell, who led UK Sport and now chairs the Youth Sport Trust. When she takes over a leadership role she asks her people three questions: "What do you do? What could you do? What's stopping you?" She sees her leadership priority as removing the organisational barriers which prevent people from being at their best.

And there is a very simple test to find out if you are an authentic leader: Look over your shoulder. Anyone there willingly? Great, you are a leader. No-one there? Guess what?

You are a leader if people choose to follow you.

is for

—

Team

"All business operations can be reduced to three words: people, product and profits. Unless you've got a good team, you can't do much with the other two."

Lee Iacocca, businessman

———

A great team with a mediocre idea wins every time over a mediocre team with a great idea, and enduringly successful leaders in any field are those who can put together world-class teams – groups of people with the collective ability to win on demand, to deliver whenever they are asked to and then some.

Any success I have had in my career is entirely down to some cunning and a lot of luck in getting some fabulous people around me.

In Liverpool, a medium-sized provincial city with a falling population, casting my leadership team was a constant struggle. It was difficult to find top talent willing to work in a social enterprise, in Liverpool, for the pay I could afford. I totally lucked out with Alison Ball though.

A Scouser through and through, Alison's emotional intelligence, passion for serious and grown up approaches to verifying our social and environmental impact and fabulous sense of humour were critical to the performance of our leadership team. The other massive thing she taught me was how to learn from failure and never to go to bed angry with anyone! She would regularly remind me that feedback is the breakfast of champions and I needed a full English every morning.

"Enduringly successful leaders in any field are those who can put together world-class teams"

At Fifteen, I was again lucky to find another great woman in Paula Dupuy who ran the restaurants and inspired everyone with her work ethic and commitment to the cause. She taught me what real grace under pressure looks like and her skills in leading the chefs, sommeliers, waiters – the whole cast which makes restaurants work – enabled me to focus on understanding and improving our social impact and new business propositions.

And don't build a team of people in your own image. The team that drives my current business Wavelength is a threesome of owners who are very different people – ages, politics, family structure, the lot. We perform really well when our different skills, experiences, capabilities, aspirations and ambitions are acknowledged and given equal weight. And this doesn't happen by chance. We invest time and money in making sure the dynamics of the team are kept healthy. It takes time, the willingness to be very honest and to know how to compromise without holding on to any resentment.

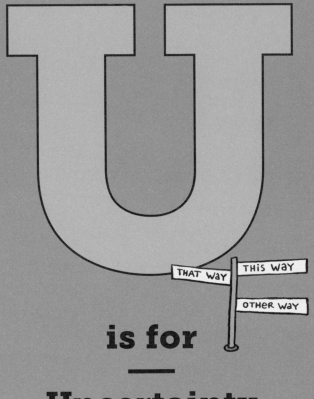

is for

—

Uncertainty

> "Nothing's for sure, that's for sure."

Anon

———

Starting and running a business will tell you a lot about yourself very quickly, especially your tolerance level for living with uncertainty and ambiguity.

If you are doing something genuinely innovative then no one has done it before and so there will be few road signs to help you. Actually not knowing what's round the corner or how your strategies will play out can be exhilarating. Indeed, approaching a challenge or problem certain you have the answer will trip you up.

As a social entrepreneur you must expect failure, success, and everything in between. But if you have a clear sense of purpose, compellingly shared with your partners, clients and employees, and you act with integrity, you will choose the right road more often than not.

And even if it turns out you went the wrong way you can still learn loads about business and social change that you can use in your next venture or job. As one of my leadership team at Fifteen used to say when I had messed it up again: "Well, we're not dead yet Liam are we?" That irrepressible sense of humour and tough-as-nails resilience were invaluable to me.

Be strong on your mission but flexible on the details of how you get there. Never pretend to people around you that you are sure of yourself when you really feel lost. Bullshitting is a terrible compass.

"Mastering the art of living creatively in ambiguity is key to your challenge as a social entrepreneur"

When living in the messiness and contradictions of starting up your social enterprise the truth is there are no flashing "This way" signs. Trusting your heart and gut is every bit as reliable (and unreliable) a strategy as obsessing over spreadsheets or spending money on consultants. I once heard a management consultant (who is actually very good) talk about the need for "pivoting around an evidence-based emergent strategy". Maybe she was being ironic and I missed it but I much prefer the less flowery and honest "making it up as you go along"!

Whatever you call it, mastering the art of living creatively in ambiguity is key to your challenge as a social entrepreneur.

is for

—

Values

> "Anyone with gumption and a sharp mind will take the measure of two things: what's said and what's done."

Seamus Heaney, poet

———

In 2001, a few years before the American energy business Enron went bankrupt – and 16 senior executives went to jail – I sat in the boardroom atop its gleaming Houston HQ.

Before the high command came in to lie to us we were shown a very high production video narrated by a Hollywood star explaining the values of the company. Over soaring orchestral music, images of Martin Luther King, Gandhi and Cesar Chavez flashed before us. This video played in Enron lifts, and all over the huge skyscraper were fabulous posters and expensive imagery trumpeting Respect, Integrity, Excellence, Communication.

Enron were superb at communicating and storytelling about their values; trouble was they weren't talking about their real values – Lying, Stealing and Corrupting Others. Those wouldn't have looked so great displayed at reception.

Your values – your core beliefs, what you stand for and hold most dear – are not what you say they are (still less what you put up on the office wall). What you really stand for is shown in your behaviour and that of your enterprise.

Your values are your beliefs in action. If you want to understand someone, don't bother too much with what they say – look at what they do – especially when they are stressed or challenged.

"What you really stand for is shown in your behaviour and that of your enterprise"

Authenticity – the alignment of what you say with what you do – is important for any business. For the social enterprise it is life and death – if indeed you want to be the change you want to see in the world.

If you don't know where you really stand, what will you do when you get knocked down?

W

is for

—

Work bloody hard

> "The fight is won or lost far away from witnesses —
> behind the lines, in the gym, and out there on the road,
> long before I dance under those lights."

Muhammad Ali, stings like a bee

———

One of the things that really struck me working in the hospitality business is just how hard people work. Long, long hours, day after day in a physically very demanding environment, on their feet for hours, rushing around. I often wonder why people do it. It's certainly not for the money.

But we can all learn from the willingness of hospitality pros to just grind it out, to keep on going, with a smile on your face, when all you want to do is go to bed (after you've dumped that cup of scalding hot coffee in the lap of that arse on table six).

Setting up and running your own enterprise can be a fantastically liberating experience – giving you deep satisfaction and pride. When it all works and your vision for your business aligns with how it actually is, well, there's nothing quite like that feeling.

But beware: getting there requires hard work, will take much longer than you ever imagined, with many dull-as-ditch-water things to be done, daily setbacks and, at the beginning certainly, many more "No's" than "Yes's" from funders and customers.

It often does feel like pushing a huge stone uphill, getting no nearer the top, with even bigger mountains on the horizon.

Whether it's furniture, food, corporate memberships, bums on seats at events, ideas, books (!) I have had to do an awful lot of sales in my time! Still do. Selling has been described as the transfer of enthusiasm and I have been able to muster tons of enthusiasm down the years. But believe me there have been many, many times when I have had to fake that enthusiasm and just step into role as the passionate, compelling social enterprise guy, just suck it up and get on with it.

"Head down. Arse up. Keep chopping"

So, when you're sitting, weeping blood from fatigue after another long day when you feel like you're getting precisely nowhere, thinking "I'll kill myself if I have to do the same sales pitch again tomorrow morning" – remember these words of wisdom which the grizzled veteran chefs pass on to the apprentices at Fifteen when they flag during a long, hot, busy service: "Head down. Arse up. Keep chopping."

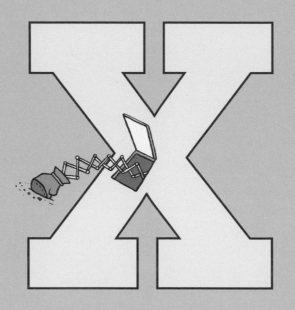

is for
—
Xtra strong resilience

"Resilience? Surround yourself with grounded dreamers, be pathalogically open to life and keep your phone charged. Red wine."

Lisa Gansky, instigator and entreprenoor

—

I like this definition of resilience I found on Google: "The property of a material that enables it to resume its original shape or position after being bent, stretched, or compressed."

Social entrepreneurship entails much bending, stretching and compression! So, how to develop this resilience? Some people clearly have more of it than others, an innate ability to roll with the blows and bounce back with a full tank. I wasn't like that in my early days. I was very chippy and every battle lost felt like the end and I often got though on willpower, running on empty, and aggression.

Partly by simply getting older and understanding that things take time and rarely go all the way you want, partly learning from my mentors, partly through the love and understanding of a great woman, I have developed more resilience and perspective on my abilities, shortcomings and blind spots.

You must uncouple your sense of self-worth from the work you do. If you believe a bad business decision means you're a bad person, or a failed initiative makes you a failure, that way lies madness or the bottle – or both.

Getting the basics of governance right is key to resilience. Yes, being in touch with your inner child is definitely going to help when bad times hit your business. But the best thing will be a great board of experienced, well informed directors who can help steer the ship through the storm. I'd rather have an experienced, cool-headed chairperson than a Zen master to call when the numbers collapse!

Don't mistake endurance or macho toughness for resilience. I have had some real hard cases in tears as they reach the end of their little, "I can take anything the world throws at me" melodrama!

Being resilient is not about being able to handle crises heroically or suffering in silence when you're in trouble. It means preparing well for the inevitable crises and getting the dull but really, really vital basics right so when the proverbial does hit the fan, your umbrella is to hand.

"Social entrepreneurship entails much bending, stretching and compression"

Resilience is built over time by having the right mentor at the right stages of your entrepreneurial journey, having lots of love in your life, getting plenty of exercise and staying healthy, nailing the bread and butter governance issues, not being stupidly reckless with money.

is for

—

Yunus

> "My greatest challenge has been to change the mindset of people.
> Mindsets play strange tricks on us.
> We see things the way our minds have instructed our eyes to see."

Professor Muhammad Yunus, social entrepreneur extraordinaire

———

I remember sitting in Liverpool reading *Banker to the Poor* for the first time as I was wrestling with all the complexities and contradictions of trying to create profitable social impact enterprises and thinking, "I'm not alone! Or mad. Look at this guy doing it at a scale I can only dream of."

Yunus is a world-class networker, hugely creative and restless for change even well into his seventies. I've been very lucky to spend time with him in recent years and many's the night when, while I've been desperate for my bed after a day of rallies, meetings at Number 10 and media interviews, there he is searching the streets looking for just one more young person to inspire and convince about social business!

He has a great facility with words and is a compelling storyteller and phrasemaker. His ability to use simple language to cut through to the chase about poverty and the structures that oppress people is a mark of that leadership calibre which attracts people to join his mission of eradicating injustice.

How compelling a vision is it that our descendants will go to what Yunus describes as 'Poverty Museums' – like we do today to Holocaust Museums – and be appalled and baffled that we for so long allowed fellow human beings to die in a world of plenty?

"Great social entrepreneurs are natural tellers of stories – many of which are true"

Telling stories to inspire, excite and mobilise people is a key skill the social entrepreneur must develop. Data and stats only get you so far in mobilising people behind you. Great social entrepreneurs tend to be people who are natural tellers of stories – many of which are true!

You need to develop the skill of telling 'future truths' – tall tales which help us get through the messiness and contradictions of the current state of our enterprises to a near future when our vision will be realised – and encourage funders and staff to stay the course with us!

I encourage you to read the speech Yunus gave when he picked up Grameen's Nobel Prize in 2006. "We get what we want," he said, "or what we don't refuse... We wanted to go to the moon. We went there. We achieve what we want to achieve. Let us join hands to give every human being a fair chance to unleash their energy and creativity." That's a narrative to get behind, isn't it?

is for

—

Zzzzz
(get plenty of sleep)

> **"A good laugh and a long sleep are the best cures in the doctor's book."**
>
> Irish proverb

———

Let me end this book of alphabetical advice to you by repeating my instruction to look after yourself. The world does not need a load more stressed out, running-on-empty social entrepreneurs. But passion, commitment, resilience, imagination – all those are badly needed.

"The world's your oyster, go for it"

According to those very smart people at Harvard – who have done experiments and everything – when we miss sleep we pay a price with our ability to process information, to learn, and our health and quality of life degrade.

So, be visionary, be bold, take risks, stay humble, get great teams and mentors round you, gather evidence, get clear about money, look after yourself, work hard. And get plenty of sleep. Simple. Good luck to you.

And, finally, here's Tommy Cooper again: "So I was getting into my car and this bloke says to me, 'Can you give me a lift?' I said, 'Sure, you look great, the world's your oyster, go for it.'"

Good luck to you.

Liam Black

Wavelength is the passion of three friends Jessica Stack, Adrian Simpson and Liam Black. Created in 2008, Wavelength's intention is to change the world for the better through business and attempts to this by working with leaders across sectors and industries to inspire, educate and connect them. Wavelength's networks run from the cutting edge of tech disruption in Silicon Valley to the villages of the rural poor in Bangladesh through the board rooms and shop floors of some of the world's most successful and admired businesses. Wavelength operates a cross subsidy business model which enables social entrepreneurs to participate in its programmes as equals with leaders from the private and corporate sectors.

thesamewavelength.com

MATTER&Co   **PIONEERS POST**

Matter&Co has built a reputation as a leading creative agency in the social innovation space. Working across the corporate, government and civil society sectors, Matter&Co creates beautiful, impactful brands, campaigns, films, events, and printed and digital communications for inspiring organisations who are passionate about purpose and use business to drive their social mission. It is also the company behind Pioneers Post, the global social enterprise magazine; the RBS SE100 Index, the market intelligence platform for social businesses, and Good Deals, the UK's leading impact investment conference.

MatterandCo.com | PioneersPost.com | SE100.net | Good-DealsUK.com